# Release it & Let it Go

Relationships & the family.

Inspirational thoughts, poems and prayers
by Theo Akpan.

Published by
MT Publishing

# Release It & Let It Go

Relationships & the family.

Copyright © 1999 by Theo Akpan
48 Cavendish Road
London N18 2LS

ISBN 0 9537661 0 1

Editor Beverley Hendricks
Illustrations by Debbie Brown.
Frontcover Concept & Photography, layout and print by
Liberty Publications Ltd., London UK

# CONTENTS

I dedicate this book
to God the Father,
God the Son
and God the Holy Spirit

May blessings be with Theo as she follows the path
the Lord has made for her.

Bishop John Francis

# INTRODUCTION

Sometimes the experiences of life can leave us with emotions and feelings that linger, evoking unpleasant memories that from time to time explode, sometimes making situations worse. We all know that feelings are better communicated especially when expressed constructively and sensitively. But before emotions and feelings can be safely released, consideration needs to be given as to what might be hindering the expressions.

One of the first steps that I needed to take in my own life was self acceptance. I struggled for many years wanting to be like my older sister. I did not know how to promote my own personal growth and I had to learn that if I was to promote the personal growth of another, then I must grow myself, I found this to be a very painful experience at times but it has also been rewarding and enriching.

As you read 'Release it and Let it Go', you will see how I struggled with my feelings, how at times I wrestled with my emotions, my strengths, weaknesses, wants, needs, mistakes and desires; trying to change my physical, mental, emotional and spiritual self to please others and then how, as my frustration intensified I discovered that the place to begin was with myself. In order for me to grow and change I had to acknowledge the importance of learning to disclose myself. I had to take the risk to show my human side, my tears, sadness, hurt, rage, pain, anger, weariness and sometimes lack of faith in myself. I realised that as I let my humanity show, others around me started to open up and as I tackled the issues within myself, other issues concerning my relationships became easier to deal with.

For many years I dealt with my feelings in ways that were not very healthy. I internalised them and was left with a sense of being trapped, guilty, hurt and even the victim of others.

There were other instances when I withdrew from everyone, denied reality, made excuses and even punished myself. When one defence system did not work I would quickly employ another. I would fluctuate between either trying to get even with people who had hurt me or accepting poor behaviour. There were other times when I was afraid of letting my feelings show, so I ignored and avoided the person or situation and forced any arising feelings away.

It is my sincere prayer that you will be able to identify with some of the issues I have faced in my life and now express in poetry. I pray that you will be able to experience a release from the hold of past experiences so that the talent, gifting and Spirit of God that is within you can flow and come forth. I pray that those of you who have spent too long a time being hard on yourselves will no longer allow others to spill their negative energy, attitudes, beliefs and pain on you and that you will throw away the burdens and unnecessary guilt, anxiety and fears.

I write to remind you that you are a gift from God. A child of God, fearfully and wonderfully made. You do not have to pretend or even try to be someone else. You have a right to enjoy and celebrate all that is good, in and around you in life, celebrating past experiences so that the present and the future can be appreciated.

Be blessed as you read.

THEO

# ABOUT THE AUTHOR

I was born on the Island of Trinidad in the Caribbean and my parents blessed me Theodora (which means gift of God). I am married to Paul and we are the delighted parents of two wonderful children, Paula and Joshua.

I had what can be described as an eventful upbringing which was rich in experiences and full of learning opportunities.

My career and ministry started within close proximity of each other. My first secular job was as a secondary school teacher and my first call to ministry was as a Sunday school teacher. My ministry as a Sunday school teacher lasted for several years and today, has left me with a passion and an intense desire to help children and youths within their family settings so that they may communicate and learn to appreciate one another.

I changed professions and became a qualified psychiatric nurse, developing my training in counselling and also working as a nurse counsellor. Within the last three years, I have progressed into management, with responsibility for teaching and training other nurses and those connected to the profession.

My Christian life became quite mundane after a while and for some years, I did not experience any spiritual or emotional growth. I suffered from the aftermath of broken relationships, family conflicts and found that I had developed a general lack of trust.

My testimony through these difficult times is that God was faithful and has been my helper. God has revealed His purpose for my life taking me step by step and stage by stage. He has also given me an anointing for prayer and as I learn to pray and spend time with Him, He is helping me to put all the pieces together for His design and is directing me as I live my life in His will and purpose.

God has given me a clear vision for ministry through writing, which is to help release people from their emotional, social, spiritual and physical bondage by tapping into the inner self to the seat of our emotions and feelings. We need to address questions on how we disclose ourselves, how to be real and how our behaviour affects those around us. We need to know when to take a stand and when to reach out and take someone by the hand.

Even as I write, the Lord is still dealing with me in some areas of my own life so you are not alone. Don't think for one moment that you are alone in having to face such issues.

The Bible says that we are overcomers and I believe that through sharing my experience with you that 'iron will sharpen iron' and you will develop better family and social relationships as well as walk in your God-given potential and purpose.

# Release It and Let It Go

I find it hard to accept him now in the way that he presents
You see I can remember all the names he called me,
The scoldings,
And other forms of punishment........
I want to let go but the memories....... they linger on.

What do I do when I find it hard to let go?
How can I not listen to what's going on inside of me?
I cannot separate from that which is a part of me.
Tell me, how can I let my true feelings show?
How can I break down my defences?
And yet come to terms with my own feelings?
I have to learn to release it and let it go.

Is it possible to control my own life
Or can I press the 'pause' button
And just hold it for a little while?
I know the answer is to form
A healthy relationship with myself,
Being aware of and accepting my own feelings;
And not be afraid to show them.
Only then will it be easier to form a relationship
With someone else.
I have to learn to release it and let it go .

What about the beliefs that I hold and the behaviours
That I have learnt?
My prejudices that influence the things that I do?
Can I really let myself experience
Positive attitudes towards others?
What about my fear of being trapped
Misused and misunderstood?
How can I release it and learn to let it go?

What do I do when I have done wrong and nobody knows?
When I want to let go because it hurts inside
and causes resentment?
What if I get caught out and have to face the shame?
What do I do with the guilt
When there is no one else to blame?
How can I release it and let it go?

What about the issues from my past, the secrets
that only God knows?
What about the pain that I still carry
from my childhood woes?
Is there a way to undo what has already been done?
How do I set myself free and move on?

I need to feel safe about my feelings as I learn
to express them.
I need to be an individual in my own right.
I cannot allow myself to be enslaved by another
Or destroyed by someone else's plight.
I must remember that it is healthy to let my feelings show.
The same thing that affects me affects the people
that I meet and know.
And healing is a process that begins with letting go.
So learn to release it and let it go


*Prayer Focus*

Lord I surrender my past hurts, pains, failures and setbacks.
I surrender my present circumstances, my mind, feelings and
emotions. I surrender my future dreams, visions and aspirations.
Help me to break ties with every negative influence of the past
and release others even as you have released me. I thank you for
my healing Lord, in Jesus name.
Amen.

# Love

Love cannot be experienced if you don't express it.
Words cannot be heard  if you don't speak.
You say you love me in your heart and I am sure
That this is true.
But love is an action word and should be demonstrated
In the things that you do.

You complain that you cannot afford presents and
Expensive gifts.
But I can get that from those who don't even like me.
I need a kind word ..., a gentle reminder...,
A loving touch..., a reassuring smile...,
Things that cannot be bought with money.

I need some of the love that you have
Locked away -
In your heart.

*Prayer Focus*

Lord help me to be a
channel of your love to
all those that you have
placed around me.
Help me to love you
with all my heart and
to love others as you
love me. Give me the
ability to love you by
my actions and my
words.
Amen.

# Love Yourself

Forgive yourself -: it is important when letting go.
Release others, those that are aware and even those
That may not know.
Let the weight drop off your shoulders.
This will generate self love and a better outlook for the future.
Loving yourself can be a wonderful adventure -
It's like learning to fly.
You take a few self empowering steps and then you push
Past the clouds as you reach for the sky.

Your love for yourself is not conditional;
It cannot be earned or bought, it has to be natural.
Do not criticise yourself, for criticism only brings resentment.
Learn to accept yourself and so discover the meaning
Of real contentment.

Discover your potential, your inner beauty and talent.
Work on your weaknesses and transform them into strengths.
Do not let your mistakes get you down.
Keep doing your best and you will find a way to go beyond.

Expand your chances for success,
Affirm the positive and let God do the rest.


Prayer Focus

Lord I thank you for my life
Teach me to be gentle with myself
and with others too.  I declare that
I am strong, blessed and  anointed
of God and that I will fulfil God's
purpose for my life .Lord I thank
you because I am full of potential
and power and in the name of Jesus
I will be able to Love myself.  Amen

# A Special Kind of Friend.

It takes a special kind of friend to sense
When you need to be alone.
To manoeuvre and come along beside you,
When you seem to have lost your way home.
Listening when you speak
Even though you're not sure what you want to say.
Encouraging when gloom lurks around,
Always pointing to a brighter day.
Weeping with you when you are sad,
Sharing your sorrows and making you glad.

Giving the best of whatever they have got.
Always willing to help when others will not.
Taking the pains to reason things out,
Rather than casting schism and doubt.
Seeks no glory for the good that they have done,
But continues steadily, contributing worthily to any cause.
Willing to forgive even when no forgiving is needed.
Gives love even when it goes unheeded.

It's a special kind of friend who sees for me
When I am blind,
Who gives to me when I cannot find,
Who understands the things I cannot explain,
Supporting and encouraging me when my courage wanes.
Who loves me not because of what I possess,
But sees in me inner virtues and so calls me blessed.
One who will stick with me until I triumph to the end

Is who I will call a special kind of friend.


(Dedicated to my dear husband Paul)

*Prayer Focus*

Lord I thank you for all the special people that you have placed in my life.  Help me to appreciate and value them. I pray that a special anointing will fall on those I love.  I pray that you will minister and meet the needs of all those who are lonely and need friendships in their life, in Jesus' name
Amen.

# People

People are the centre of everything we say and do
The How! Why and even the way we relate.
Our very existence depends on our human relationships
And our ability to communicate.

As people, we are different and complex
In our own unique ways.
We may look alike yet be very different.
We may speak the same language
yet still not understand each other.
We may listen to the same conversation
Yet not hear the same things.

As an individual, I have my own perception
And issues that I carry,
The things I like, the things I do not like,
The people that I can relate to,
the ones I would rather not associate with.
Sometimes I have to make a conscious effort
To put aside my own prejudices
And treat people as humans -
With compassion -
Showing God's love and kindness

I often have to stop and address the issue of diversity,
Take a closer look at man and see each one separately.
This can be at times interesting
And sometimes quite complex
As I learn to identify with others in their circumstance
And so put relationships in the right context.

People tend to treat you depending on how
They manage their own inner issues.
Some will welcome and embrace you,
Others just ignore all clues.

Some will love you today and tomorrow,
They will pass you on their way.
There  seems to be little indication
As to how people may react.

I have found that it is wise to leave room
For those who will not understand.
I aim to give more than I get.
I am learning to accept less than I expect.
I need to be realistic, face the facts and ignore the fantasy
Care for others in all that I do, always remembering
That people need people and that includes me and you.


*Prayer focus*

Lord I thank you for the wisdom to deal with people, use me as an
instrument of peace that will  minister healing and deliverance in
the places you would have me to go.  Lord help me to be sensitive
to the needs of others, offering help where I can so that tests
might be turned into testimonies for your glory, Lord.
Thank you Lord for opportunities to be a blessing, building people
up rather than tearing them down. In the name of Jesus I pray.
Amen.

# Family

I am a member of a large family with issues vast and wide.
How can I separate my own issues from my family issues?
And not get swallowed up with the tide?
I feel powerless and helpless
When I look at the deeper issues
Like drug addiction, addiction to pain, suffering,
Victimisation, with no motivation to change.
Then there are the unresolved issues like abuse,
The family members that are too controlling
And the ones that make too little contact.

In order for me to survive the family
I have had to exercise my individual right.
I have a right to my own feelings, thinking and behaving
I have a right to be happy and enjoy a life that's fulfilling.

I will be sensitive to their needs  and acknowledge their fears
But I do not need to take on and carry their burdens
to show that I care.

I am learning to detach in love from
Family members and their issues.
I have a responsibility to allow myself
Room for personal growth.
Taking my own personal space does not mean
That I do not love my family
And should never be interpreted as lack of care.
I am simply addressing my own issues
And giving them the space to address theirs too.

I am learning to strike a balance by separating
The issues that are mine
And the ones that are not.

I want to stand up for my family but I am careful
That they may need me too much.
I want to be there for them but I'm mindful
That they may become over-dependent.

Sometimes I feel that there is a gulf between myself
And some members of my family.
Sometimes I feel tempted to physically
Pull them over with me.
I know this cannot be done,
Each person must come by choice.
The reality is that some will come and some will not;
The choice is not mine.

However, I must continue to live in the light
And pray and believe that the ones I love
Will follow me one day.


*Prayer Focus*

Father today I stand in the gap for my family and I
repent on our behalf I confess the sin
of _____ (name your family sins)
and I thank you for breaking the cycle
of sin, sickness, poverty and lack.
I thank you for saving us from
ourselves and from the
destruction of the enemy.
I take back everything
the enemy has stolen
from my family and
I declare freedom
and salvation
in Jesus' name.
Amen.

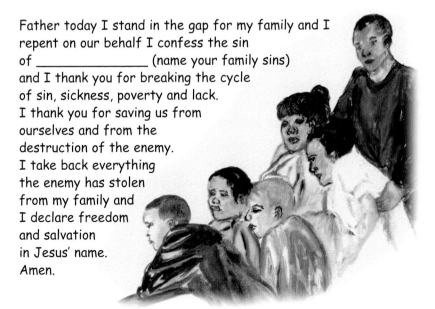

# When things go wrong

I am sure I did it right but somehow it turned out wrong.
It didn't work for me this time.
I had given this individual a lot of support as she struggled
To cope with her problems.
The sleepless night of anxiety and worry had drained her
Emotionally.
Her inability to pray and the lack of faith had left her
Spiritually empty.

I saw her need and volunteered to help,
I used a lot of time, energy and effort in the process.
I stuck with her until she finally came through.
And then things changed.

She became overly dependent on me and expected me
To meet her every need.
She invaded my personal space, made demands
On my time and person.

As the reality of the situation came home to me
I took a step back to reflect on the pattern
Of relationships in my life.
There have been times when I have been stuck
And tried too hard or not hard enough
There were other times when it was crucial for me
Not to give up and keep trying harder
Then there were instances when it was necessary to let go,
Detach and stop trying so hard.
When some relationships do not work,
It's usually God trying to tell us something.

I have learnt that I should not force myself on others
Because I could be used, or suffer rejection.
As I cut myself and the other person free, another
Relationship — a more promising one, may open for me.
I have had to learn to let go of my frustration, anxiety and
Desperation before I could receive peace.
I needed to wait and trust God for guidance.
Things may sometimes go wrong no matter what you do,
But in order to overcome we need
To trust God for the future
And not take things personally.

So, what do you do  when things go wrong?

The answer points back to letting go!


*Prayer focus*

Lord teach me to trust you
at all times.
Help me to be rooted and
grounded in your steadfast
love.
Help me to be focused on
your will and purpose
for my life.
Anoint me to stand every
test and overcome
every hurdle, in Jesus'
name. Amen

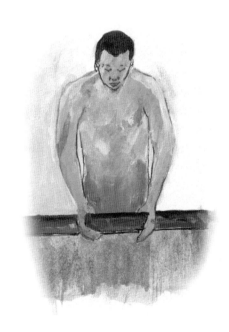

# Pain

What do you do when you feel pain?
Someone I trusted had lied about me,
Someone in whom I had invested my time and energy.
Someone in whom I believed I had a good relationship with
And had extended my hand as one would to a friend.
Then the time came for that friendship to be tested.
The potential for personal gain was great and our
Relationship could not withstand the test.

My friend chose what seemed to be the easier option
And ditched me,
Giving priority to money and choosing
To be associated with influential company.
I suffered alone.
The pain was intense physically, my shoulders ached.
Emotionally, I felt tired and drained
From the weight of the pain.
I had to learn to listen to myself and identify
Why it hurt so much in the first place.
I addressed the issue of expectation from others
Dealing with reality and meeting my own needs.
Then I had to make the next step, which was
Learning to share my pain.
This was difficult as I felt vulnerable
And was afraid to open up again.

I attended church as usual on Sunday,
I was hoping for some form of release.
As I started to pray and praise,
The Spirit of the Lord came upon me.
The tears flowed down my cheeks, then I started to cry
Then scream ... my release had come .
The pain I felt had stopped, I just needed to rejoice
For my breakthrough and move forward in God.

Prayer Focus

Father help me accept the reality of pain. Help me to be better and not bitter. Lord heal me of every mental, physical and emotional scar in Jesus' name.
Thank you for the ability to focus on you and not the circumstances.
Thank you for the ability to press and push past in Jesus' name. Amen.

# Intimacy

I had a conversation with a relative today
And it was really enlightening.
She was warm, intelligent and very accommodating.
She did not present herself in a way I expected her to.
On reflection, I had to accept
That I had been wrong this time.
For months and possible years
I had avoided her as a person.
I had listened to the many tales about her
And had gone along with the majority view.

I was afraid to let myself get close.
I sabotaged the relationship
Every time it moved to a level of closeness and intimacy.
I used criticism to create a distance that allowed me
To feel safe.
I exaggerated her character deficits and denied her needs
And mine in the process.

The truth is I was not available for intimacy ,
I was afraid  of losing myself.
Worried that someone else would have power over me.
I had to learn that it was okay
to let myself get close to people.
I needed to make safe boundaries
And let myself be who I am.
And let others be who they are
And enjoy the bond of that
Easy feeling between us.

*Prayer Focus*

Lord help me to be me and not allow myself to be led and influenced by others. Help me to think, pray and make decisions based on facts and guided by the Holy Spirit.
Father I thank you for a new level of anointing and awareness.
I thank you for the maturity to give and receive love in Jesus name.
Amen.

# I must

I must think thoughts that are pure and good
Never forgetting the things that I learnt in
My early childhood.
The days that I spent with dear Grandmother
Makes me wish that they were still here.
She was a real good- natured soul
With very few others like her in this world
She took time to laugh, and played with us too
Taught us to cook, clean and do our household dues.
We went fishing along the river,
Relaxing and enjoying God's creation and nature.

My grandmother is now aged and going on in years
The love that she shared will always be remembered.
The joy, sorrow and even the tears
I must never forget my teenage years,
The pranks that I played and my meandering ways
The beautiful countryside, where as a child I lived
Amidst poverty and difficulties that adverse
Circumstances give,

I learnt values while I was young
Respect, discipline, honesty, and the difference between
Right and wrong.
I completed high school, only God knows how!
It was inconceivable, but I had started on my journey of
Success now.
I must never forget the generous and well intentioned ones
Who contributed somehow
By giving their best, however small.

Now I have a duty to perform
To help others in their quest for self advancement
Letting them know that there is room at the top
For those who will cultivate a sense of achievement.
I must end my writing now
But always remember, if you strive for mastery, you'll find
It somehow.


(Dedicated to my dear Grandmother Doris Thomas who died in 1999)


*Prayer Focus*

Thank you Lord for all
the wonderful people
who you have
caused to enrich my life
Help me to extend the
love caring
and help that was
extended to me. Help me
to bless others and not
to take them for
granted,
in Jesus' name, Amen.

# Peer Pressure

There are a lot of distractions in our society today.
Most of it keep us from focusing on living the Bible way.
Take one glance at society's dismay.
Check out the trends and the things that they say.

Just who are the deviants?
Is it the young people who are taking drugs,
Or the young people who are not?

There is such pressure in our society today.
One person tries to persuade the other to go the wrong way.
In heaven's name, how can they resist the pressure?
Friends may think that they are nothing but misfits.
Parents have not got a clue as to what they can do about it.
Folks may have ambitious plans for me,
But it is their dream and has nothing to do with my reality.
It seems fashionable and reasonable to be with the crowd.
It is tempting and alluring to just join the mob.

The risk is too great, my dear boy.
Life has its stages and you must overcome pressure
If you will grow to be tall.
You will never be fulfilled until you become
All that you can be.
So press in to God and take hold of your destiny.
God has a plan of good and means you well.
So stay tuned to Him and the Spirit of God
Will cause you to excel.

## Prayer Focus

Lord I thank you for calling me as a youth. I thank you that I will walk in my God given potential and power.
I shield every youth from the influence of the evil one.
I come against intimidation, bullying, poor self-esteem, sexual sins, lack of focus, and vision. I bless every youth and I thank you that we will accomplish the great plans that you have for our lives in Jesus' name. Amen

# Care for the Children.

Children are a heritage of the Lord.
They are loaned to their parents and are dear to God.

This world can sometimes be a cruel place
So they need someone to guide and lead them to grace.

What happens to them now, will determine
what the future brings.
Speak good over them,
Bless and cover them,
Be an example in Godly things.

The first responsibility is to the family
Mum, Dad, brother, sister, uncle, aunt
And Christian brethren.
Just be an example, whatever you do.

Our children are the next generation
Out of them should come Ministers, Presidents
And Leaders of nations.
In every girl, there is a woman
In every boy, there is a man,
Open to influence and needing to be established
In God's divine plan.
One day certainly, they'll grow up for true.
What they turn out to be, will depend largely on you.
Give them good guidance
And they'll grow up to Bless you.

(Dedicated to my children Paula and Joshua)

*Prayer Focus*

Lord I thank you for my own children and every other child whose life I am able to influence . I affirm that they will emerge as great leaders, successful business men and women, professionals, pastors and ministers in governments and churches. I cover them from the ills of society, illicit drugs, promiscuity, false religions and satanic influences. I shield them from peer pressure and bullying. I command an anointing upon them, to walk in obedience to you Lord in Jesus' name . Amen.

# The teenage conflict.

The river of youth beams with activity.
It's full of excitement and fun lovers
looking for the next party.
It is only a few who will sit quietly
And contemplate God's will.
As there is always something new
Another opportunity for a thrill.

Biologically, adolescence is a very challenging time
As hormones are activated stimulating growth,
Development and curiosity of mind.
Physically the body develops, hair grows,
The voice breaks,
Pimples appear and disappear
And external growth takes place.
Mentally, the ability to reason and think independently
Becomes stronger,
With more emphasis on 'my' and 'why'
As the limitations decrease.
Spiritually, questions are asked
As demands for knowledge and understanding increase.
Emotionally, there is self exposure,
With the ability to find their identities
And take new initiatives.

There are many situations to which
The teenagers must take heed.
They can face life with courage or look to others
To meet their needs.
If you give them your time, support and God given ability,
You will build lives and characters that will produce
Men and women of destiny.

*Prayer Focus*

Dear Lord give me the wisdom that will enable me to know and do what is right. Give me wisdom beyond my years.
Give me the capacity to learn and understand your ways.
Help me to honour and respect my parents, adults and those in authority; help me to be a leader rather than a follower of the crowd.
Lord I pray for a spirit of excellence upon all youths.
I declare that God's wisdom and anointing will operate in their lives and they will be the head and not the tail in Jesus Name. Amen.

# Somebody Loves Me

My mother died when I was only three.
My dad re-married and lost touch with his little girl.
My step mother was too self centred
to see beyond her own goals.
And so I existed in 'No-man's' world.

My paternal brother and sister did not seem to be
in touch with reality.
Both their parents were alive and pampered them with plenty.
I spent many tearful days thinking of how the world
had cheated me in so many, many ways.

I was invited to Sunday school by a very kind friend
Who said: 'Somebody loves you and he will make amends'.
I couldn't understand it.
The pain inside me clouded my vision of success
and my ability to overcome.

I was in a world of my own
There was no one I felt I could trust.

I had fellowship with sadness, hate, bitterness,
pain and disgust.
I felt they had lived with me for all my young life.
I didn't want to loose them,
I felt I could not pay the price.

I argued, debated, contemplated, reasoned and then
reluctantly accepted Christ.
The joy was overwhelming
No words could express it.
Now I live in hope
Coupled by a life that's honoured and blessed.

(This poem reflects the struggles of a Sunday School child after the loss of her mother)


*Prayer Focus*
Dear Lord thank you for your love which is now shed abroad in my heart.
I pray that I will be able to minister and pass on that love to others, even as you have blessed me Lord.
I thank you for healing me of my past pain. I pray that I will be an instrument of healing to others too. I bless you Lord because I know that it is you who has started a good work in me and you are able to complete it. in Jesus' name. Amen.

# Parents

It's the parents' role to surround their children
With an atmosphere of love, self control
And a sense of responsibility.
It's imperative that the parents mould the child
And inspire him in God's plan of authority.
In order for your child to know God,
Parents believe me, you must know Him yourself
And be submitted to Him completely.

Undoubtedly they are cute, gorgeous lovely little things.
Love them we must, but be prepared for the challenges
That their life brings.
Even toddlers exercise that ability to deceive.
They acknowledge mother's presence
And quickly stop the wrong.
But reach for it again once that presence is gone.
You see we were all born in sin and shaped in iniquity,
The Bible says.
So we need to exercise diligence and discipline
When our children disobey.
'How do I discipline a child that I love?' One parent asks.
Mix it with love and it will bear fruit that will last.

Some children may need special help
And even some parents too.
Mothers never compromise your craving for love
From your child with fear of rejection whatever you do.
We must have high expectation and reasonable standards,
Be able to acknowledge wrong, apologise, verbalise
And give honour to men as fathers.

Pray for your children everyday,
Faithfully present them to the Almighty
And they will grow up to be men and women of integrity,
Influencing our society.


*Prayer Focus*

Lord I pray for my partner and myself that we will be a Godly
influence to our children.
I cancel every seed that the enemy has planted in our home.
I cover our children with the blood of Jesus against every
ungodly influence.
I thank you for wisdom to raise them with love and to be a
good example to them.
I pray for a special anointing on the parents to meet the
individual needs of every child in Jesus' name . Amen.

# Mother

A peaceful spirit and a sweet voice,
A life of sacrifice with very little choice.
Her service was always in demand,
But not always appreciated,
As her labour of love was not always reciprocated.
A mother holds the reins with such serene hands,
Confronting darkness, planting seeds of life
With vigour and radiance.

Mother influences more by what is done, than what is said.
Her beauty and enchantment is what attracts,
Dispelling fear and dread.
A wise woman builds up her house the, Bible says,
Trains her children well and guides them in the kings way.
She takes counsel from the Word,
Keeps away from gossip and whispers that can
Sometimes be heard.

She plants seeds that would one day grow into fruit.
Fruit that would last and be an emblem of youth.
She works on herself her weaknesses,
Failures and shortcomings too.
Represents good in whatever she does,
Has a spirit of excellence and reverence in the house of God.
Is faithful and invests time with the Lord
Her children will grow up to bless her no doubt,
As the Lord greatly increases and brings her out.

## Prayer Focus

I thank you Lord
that my children
shall rise up and call
me blessed.
By faith I declare
that my family will
stay together.
I pray that your
beauty within me will
beautify my home,
my husband, my
children and my
world.
I thank you for
divine favour and the
capacity to love and
be a true mother.
in Jesus' name Amen.

# Men

Where are the men in our churches today?
There are some boys in Sunday school,
But after a while, they tend to go another way.
There is a deficit in the house of God.

Something must be done to correct the situations.
We need men who will be men and take their rightful place
In this nation.
The sisters are often left to get on with the men's task,
Bringing up children, coping with neglect and brothers -
This is no farce.

Why do our men function below their full capacity?
Is it because of the mothers and sisters,
Who rule so dominantly?
After having been forced to compensate
For the lack of male authority?
For the sisters this may be a simple act of survival
And self preservation.
Suppressing the pain, and leaving little room for repetition.

The whole world is affected by this misdemeanour.
Brothers stand up and be counted.
Take your place and recognise that you are
Desperately needed, not just wanted.
Man was created for the glory of God
To manifest God's nature and image
And be the authority in the Lord.

Remember men,
The woman will glory in her relationship with her man ,
If he takes responsibility to lead her by the hand.

## Prayer Focus

I declare that the men will rise up as a mighty army in this land
and assume their role as fathers and leaders of this nation.
I speak a blessing over the men and come against every stronghold
of the enemy.
I thank you Lord for breaking the chains that hold them
captive and for setting our men free, in Jesus' name, Amen.

# Elusive Love

My heart had been captured, no doubt!
I could not refuse when he offered to take me out.
He was a kind and compassionate man
With a unique sense of value coupled with charisma and charm.
There was no need to pretend to be someone else.
He was so reassuring and accepting
That I was just propelled into being myself.
I enjoyed being childish and frivolous in His company,
But exerted strength and courage when I had to be womanly.

It had not been very long when our happy interlude
Was abruptly, interrupted.
Fate demanded that our dreams be indecisively halted.
It was with a bitter-sweet sensation,
That he eventually departed.
Leaving behind a love that was jeopardised
Too soon after being started.
Undoubtedly he had helped me in the past.
Only God knows why it did not last.
I cried myself to sleep, weeping many a tear
Still hoping that he'll come back with the years.
I devised a plan to protect myself from a love
that was so intense,
Not perceiving that it was an emotion born out of need,
An issue which I needed to address.

Then one day it suddenly dawned on me,
I said to myself after all, maybe, that was not meant to be.
I publicly concealed my hurt and pain,
Deciding to start all over again.
Striving to suppress my inner turmoil
I reasoned and rationalised
Still hoping it would be realised by God above
What's done is already done, a poet once said,

But maybe just this once
Could it be that love was not lost in this instance.

Now I look back and wonder why I punished myself
As I struggled outside of God.
I denied my feelings the fear, the need the pain
And even the truth in the process.
I did not think it was okay, neither did I feel safe
Nor confident about my emotions to express.
I did not want to be judged so I repressed my feelings
And memories.
I was hurting inside but I suffered in silence.
I destroyed my self esteem, confidence and sense of worth
Stunting my development and preventing personal growth.

Now I know that love is a beautiful experience.
However it must be built on the right foundations —
Love for self and God and then love can be rewarding
And meaningful.


*Prayer Focus*

Lord help me to never again evade the love that you have for me.
Help me to put you first in my life and allow you to add all things to
me. Help me to trust when I feel afraid, Lord. I come against
every spirit of confusion that tries to upset the peace that you
have given to me.
I pray for those who
are at cross roads in
their life that you will
order their steps and
establish them in your
will. Thank you God
for plans to prosper
and not hurt me. in
Jesus' name, Amen.

43

# Attitude

Have you ever stopped to consider what attitude
Is all about?
I have found out that it comprises of thoughts,
Feelings and moods.
My attitude tends to affect my perception.
My perception then influences my behaviour and the way
I relate to others.
My behaviour demonstrates how I think and feel about you.
Attitudes are contagious whether good or bad.
Jesus began to preach in His own hometown.
He received negative attitudes and the Scriptures say
This affected His function.

If you want to treat others well then you need to do
What the Bible says.
Think on pure and wholesome thoughts
As you organise your days.
Begin to act them out for the good of you and me.
As you act them out you will be displaying positive attitudes
For all to see.
What you sow you will reap,
So invest in your relationship with others
And you will be rewarded with friendship.

Is it possible for me to change my attitude?
How can I be a bit more positive?
How can I stop keeping others and myself down?
How can I acquire an attitude that delivers and sets others
free from doing wrong?
How do I get the same attitude that Jesus had?

The Bible says let the same attitude that is in Christ
Be also in you.
But that depends on the things I say and do.
The Bible implies that my attitude can be adjusted.
I can take on the mind of Christ, influence my behaviour
And then dictate to my circumstances.

Remember the only difference between somebody who wins
And somebody who loses is their attitude.


*Prayer Focus*

Thank you Lord for helping me to have a positive attitude. One
that will help me to influence others and glorify you. Help me to
uproot the negative attitudes of the past and reveal every negative
attitude that is shutting the door against me.
Cause me to be a blessing and not a stumbling block. Thank you
Lord for renewing my attitude and causing me to challenge others
to a higher life in you. In the name of Jesus.  Amen.

# Change

Change lies at the centre
Of the most challenging
Cross-roads in life.
If managed appropriately,
It can lead to fulfilment
And help to reduce strife.
When handled properly,
It can lead to
Self development,
Promotion and
A meaningful life.
Change, when rejected,
Procrastinated and ignored
Can lead to a lack of
Fulfilment, stagnation
And strife.

You can change your life if you are willing
To change your thinking.
Your thoughts can be influenced by your experience,
Your past development and learning.
Your views can be biased, prejudiced
And bear no relation to facts.
It can be affected by improper forms of relationship
That create a need for self awareness, training, Development
and strong leadership.

After I was confronted with the truth of God's Word
I felt exposed.
I tried to cover up my conviction
By branding all Christians hypocrites.
I highlighted their faults and shortcomings
Because I did not want to look at myself.

It was hard to accept that I was wrong
About my concept of God and self.
Accepting that I was wrong meant I would have to change
I was comfortable with the way I was.
I didn't want to change because change meant losing control.

Do you listen to what you say?
How can you be sure it cannot be done another way?
Are your views rigid?
Are your beliefs unshakeable?
Are they based on facts, myths or reality?
Life is a journey with many stages to cross
You must be prepared to develop,
Even in your attitudes and thoughts
Learn from your past, don't let it hold you down.
Look to the future and be prepared to move on.
Do not discard your experiences, for they are valuable
And should be made to last.

However you must release the patterns that keep you
Living in the past.
Do not rob yourself of God's ultimate call.
Release the fear and anxiety and give Jesus your all
Your blessing is just around the corner
So remove the mask, allow Jesus to bless and honour.


*Prayer Focus*


Lord I pray for divine help this day. I acknowledge my limitations :
those that I have allowed others to place on me, and those that I
have placed on myself. I thank you for the grace to receive
transformation in every area of my life. I pull down every
stronghold of my mind, I submit everything in me that resists your
Word and your will and I thank you for breakthrough this day in
Jesus' name.
Amen.

# Secrets

Secrets can be a virtue as well as a curse
When treasured deep in the heart,
From those you love the most.
Most times, we guard those seemingly hideous things
Hoping to protect our loved ones from the danger
That it supposedly brings.
But it always never works out that way
Almost as if by instinct intruding on an inopportune day.

Secrets can have bitter re-percussions,
Ending in broken relationships and defiant mistrust,
Leaving very little room for discussion.
It can have very negative undertones,
Leaving many hearts bemoaning and lamenting -
If only I had known.

There is also the issue of confidentiality
Where I entrust my inner thoughts and feelings
Hoping to find empathy.
This has been very helpful for me in the past
My burden lightened, I was able to take off the mask.

There are some hurts that cannot be carried alone.
They can over burden, oppress and lead you to moan.
It is comforting to have a shoulder to lean on.
Two is better when one is not so strong.
Obviously, somethings are better left unsaid
When circumstances that threaten appear to be dread.
There are times when judgement and good sense must prevail.
And if I would be wise to my tongue I must put a veil.

Keeping secrets can be viewed as good and bad,
Depending on the experiences that one has had..
Talk when you must. I would say first, be tactful
Always do it in a diplomatic way.

*Prayer Focus*

Father you know the dark secret of my
heart. The things that come between me
and you and others too. Help me to be
honest and true to myself and to you.
Lord I open up to thee and I thank you
for a new confidence to trust you.
I break free from every tendency that
is contrary to the Spirit of God.
I cover the body of Christ with a spirit
of freedom from bondages and yokes of
intimidation, insecurity and fear.
I speak a new anointing of boldness,
liberty , understanding, wisdom and
clear channels of communication in the
body of Christ, in Jesus' name,
Amen.

# The Child in Me

I am a person too, you know!
Young in age but full of potential and rearing to go.
'Ask questions to be wise' , someone said.

'Sh...sh...sh..Be quiet ! Little girls must be seen
And not heard'.
The world appears to be such a confused place.
Everyone seems to be running, but going no place.
I tried to talk to my teacher today.
She completely evaded the issue,
Referring me on to another along life way.

Tell me,
Why is my body made up this way?
Why am I a boy and not a girl?
Why am I thin and not fat?
Why am I white and not black?
There must be an answer to all of life's questions.

Yes, it's found in the Lord who created us unique and special
With ability to think, decide and actualise
Our God -given potential.
The child in me wants to develop and grow.
So, answer my question and empower me
So that I too will learn and know.

## Prayer Focus

I thank you Lord for setting me free from every emotional baggage and bondage of insecurity and rejection. I come against everything that tries to belittle and put me down. I thank you Lord that I am now free to honour and praise you. I pray for families at this time and thank you for a new level of acceptance, respect, recognition, love, understanding and support within the family unit. I come against every device of the enemy. I declare stability, individual growth and development in the family, in Jesus' name. Amen.

# Assumptions.

What did you say....?
You thought ....
How could you assume?
Well...... I didn't realise.
You look a bit quiet, uncertain, simple to say the least.
Don't assume.
God uses the simple things to confound the wise.
Often, the ones who talk a lot do so in an attempt
To cover and disguise.

Excuse me, has the Lord spoken to you lately?
Have you been spending time with Him?
Have you taken time to pray for me?
How do you know what His purpose and vision for my life is?
How do you know God's heart for me?
How do you arrive at your conclusions?
Are you looking at the externals and the things you see?
Do you have any idea what is God's will for me?
If the answer is no then take a step back.
Allow the Holy Spirit to complete His work.

He who started the good work in me is able to complete it.
What I need is those who would stand with me;
To destroy the works of the enemy.
Did you realise that the enemy had placed
A Satanic embargo on my life?
Just recently he was monitoring my every movement,
Blocking my progress accusing and bombarding me.
You see satan too works under assumptions.
He assumes that if he keeps up the pressure,
I will eventually succumb.
But I am in a battle in which I am destined to overcome.

You need to decide which side you are on,
Then make the necessary adjustments and move on.
We speculate about this, that and the other,
Think unkind thoughts about one another.
Why not become each others cover
And stand in the gap for one another
We are not meant to cause each other pain
God intended us to be a strong force that would encourage
And not pass blame.
Do not assume that things are the way they look
You need to take time off and read the page of The Book.
Do not think you know it better than anyone else could
Learn to differentiate between evil and good.
How did you arrive at your destination?
Were you born into the position?
The same God that watches over you cares for others too.
The simple, the sophisticated even those that are untrue.
God is Lord of all and that includes you and I.


*Prayer Focus*

Lord help me to see through your eyes. Help me to hear what you
are saying. Give me the ability to make the right decisions and
choices. Help me to remain focused on your will and your purpose.
Bless me Lord
and help me
to be a
blessing to
others. Help
me not to
judge others
so that I may
not be judged
in return. in
Jesus' name.
Amen.

# Living Today

What would you like to happen in your life today?
Tomorrow or at a future date?
What are you hoping to accomplish or striving to attain?
Are they big things or little things?
What are the areas of development that you will like to see?
Where would you like to go?
What would you like to be?
Do you have character deficits that you will like to improve?
Do you recognise the need to change?
Are there bad habits that need to be removed?
There is often disharmony in our relationship
With self and others.
Everything you do and say has an impact
On the life of another.

Why are the youths often judged by the older folks?
Ostracised and burdened with unnecessary yokes?
Because no time is taken to build meaningful relationships
Prevent life's pitfalls and unintended slips.
It takes patience and consistency
To learn the lessons of life.
Some of the most valuable lessons in life
Have to be repeated time after time,
So that we might avoid mistakes and loss.

Society today makes demands, which means
That we often put pressure on each other.
But behaviour takes time to change and form
So we need to stop all the fuss and bother.
It takes time for young people to learn, live
And appreciate life's benefits.
This can only happen in an environment
Of a loving and caring relationship.
We need to spend time in other peoples' territory,

Listen to their cries, share their joy, laughter and pain.
For if we are to help, then this is mandatory.
We must do our own part in living our own life,
Live for the present moment,
Let go of our fears, anxiety and strife.
We must set goals, as they give our life direction.
Trust God as our source and the core of our very foundation.

(Dedicated to my former Sunday School children of Arima Trinidad West Indies)

*Prayer Focus*

Lord I break
every negative tie
of the past in my
life.
Lord help me to
live in the present.
I thank you for
anointing me with
wisdom, and the
ability to pass on
to others the
lessons I have
learned. Thank you
Lord for helping
me to grow,
mature and
develop myself
and others around
me. in Jesus' name.
Amen.

# Let Life be a blessing.

My life is one of those blessings
That I need to thank God for.
I need to stop and capture the beauty of the roses,
Enjoy and welcome the chatter of my children.
There are times when I've allowed myself to walk around
With worry and depression.
Now with God's power, I will exchange it for laughter
And freedom of expression.
Today as I look around, I can find numerous things
For which I can be thankful.

In order to enjoy life, I need to cultivate a heart
That's grateful.
I will withdraw from the deposit of joy, love and peace
Which the Spirit has placed within me.
I need to tap into my inner resource and draw from it.
As I do, I believe I will be blessed and be able
To bless those around me.
I need to block out the influences that rob me
Of my peace of mind.
I need to treat myself well, be loving and kind
I need to experience good feelings about myself,
And humankind.

I need to acknowledge the virtue of taking
One step at a time.
I will make every day a good day.
Face the challenges,
Learn and improve.
I will choose not to worry about what will happen tomorrow
If I laugh too much today.

Lord teach me to enjoy life and spread sunshine to others
along the way.

*Prayer focus.*

Father help me to be a blessing to others and to allow others
to bless me too.
Help me to enjoy the beauty of nature and all of your creation that
you have blessed us with.
Thank you Lord for being healthy, physically,
mentally and emotionally.
Thank you Lord for your gift of love, power and a sound mind, in
Jesus' name. Amen

Extract from Theo's next book 'Christ and the People of God'.

# Motive

What motivated you to do what you did?
Was it love and a need to honour and give?
Was it your desire to build and not to pull down?
Was the purpose to encourage
and empower another to be strong?

Why did you act so hastily?
You refused to listen and demonstrated very little care.
It was the first time I had spoken out in a group.
I was anxious my voice quivered but you did not hear.

I was full of the zeal of the Lord and really wanted
to spread the fire.
I spoke openly and honestly from a heart of desire.
But you cross-examined every word,
Challenged, opposed and then left me for dead.
I wonder what really was on your mind.
Was it my issue or yours?
Tell me what made you so blind.

Did you ever stop to question
Why that person complained to you?
Was it because of their insecurities, complexes
Or the condition of their heart?
Was it an opportunity to exaggerate
Or even to appear to be smart?
Did you handle the situation with maturity
Or did you stop to take sides?
Did you look at it in its proper context

Or did you judge because what you heard
Made you so vexed?

The Book of Proverbs exhorts us to be quick to hear
And slow to speak.
Doing otherwise will only bring defeat.
You can never know what is in another man's heart,
So leave the judgement to God and focus on your purpose,
Aiming always to fulfil your part.

Stay in touch. Should you wish to be kept informed of further publications by Theo please write with your details to:

M.T. Publishing
48 Cavendish Road
Edmonton
London N18 2LS

God bless you.